Southern Hospitality
at Home

Southern Hospitality
at Home

The Art of Gracious Living

Susan Sully

RIZZOLI
NEW YORK

New York · Paris · London · Milan

When you've produced a touch of luxury,
a touch of style, and possibly a sense of happy
anticipation, your guests will begin to feel that
maybe they are going to be spoiled a bit.

MRS. EMILY WHALEY
Mrs. Whaley Entertains, 1998

CONTENTS

INTRODUCTION

The words "Southern hospitality" instantly conjure a cornucopia of images, textures, tastes, scents, and sounds: porches with white columns; a wide front door layered with a pentimento of antique paint; the spicy-sweet scent of jasmine; iced tea or juleps spiked with backyard mint; the sound of a voice with lingering vowels saying, "Come on in." And that's just a short list. While every region has its own brand of hospitality, only the South's is so legendary and distinctive. But why? Historical accounts written by foreign visitors contain awed descriptions of lavish feasts and rustic entertainments, rooms appointed with English silver and French porcelain, and, most important of all, ready invitations to acquaintances and strangers alike to join a party or spend the night. Some attribute this tradition of graciousness to the fact that the South was, outside of major cities, sparsely populated in its early days. A developing region isolated from the cosmopolitan society its early residents knew and missed, it was composed of enormous plantations interspersed with stretches of wilderness that made travel arduous. Neighboring folk on the way from here to yonder in the intense Southern heat required a place to quench their thirst and dally in the shade. Visitors making longer trips, traveling a day or more to get from one destination to the next, needed a place to lay their heads and rest their horses.

The gracious treatment of an uninvited stranger or unexpected guest is the ultimate expression of hospitality and one that is deeply rooted in the South. In the more populous early-American settlements in the North, doors were not always opened as quickly nor such generous reception bestowed upon unknown visitors. "What makes Southern hospitality as I know it comes from a rural perspective," says Alabama-born architect Bobby McAlpine, "the living in a small place in the country that wasn't really a destination for anybody. Somebody coming to see you was something you were starved for; it gave you a reason to inventory and see what you had to offer. It brought out the bountiful in you that the everyday doesn't necessarily bring." This recollection of twentieth-century Southern society applies even more so to life in the early and post–Civil War South, where both rural and urban residents relished the coming of visitors from afar and the news of family and friends, current fashions and affairs, and fresh conversation they brought.

Impressions from centuries-old letters and diaries recorded in Jennie Holton Fant's *The Travelers' Charleston* offer many descriptions of the warm welcome voyagers enjoyed. Upon touring a plantation midway between Charleston and Savannah in 1828, Scotswoman Margaret Hunter Hall wrote, "The more we saw of the house, the more did our inclination to remain increase. . . . On the first floor is a small drawing-room and dining room opening upon a deep piazza as they call them here. From this piazza a few steps lead down to a delightful garden filled with all sorts of flowers in full bloom. . . ." Moving from the enticements of house and garden to the table, she describes a meal composed of boiled rice, hashed turkey, broiled quails, and "Indian corn flour . . . made into cakes of every description, each more delicious than the other." And that was only breakfast—a more than ample meal served to a pair of travelers hitherto unknown by their hosts. "Assuredly we must allow the virtue of hospitality to its full extent to these planters, for it is quite common for strangers to go to their houses in the way we have come here."

THE BOUNTIFUL TABLE

In 1839, another Scottish traveler described a Charleston entertainment he attended in "a very handsome house of some antiquity, the rooms fitted up with figured wainscot in the old English style. Twenty persons sat down to dinner at about half-past four o'clock. We had a most abundant feast, of which I mention the particulars merely to show the style of such a dinner here." The vast spread laid out on the long mahogany table included "turtle-soup, fish, venison, boiled mutton, roast turkey, boiled turkey, a ham, two boiled salted tongues, two tame ducks, two wild ducks, some dressed dishes, boiled rice, hominy, potatoes, cauliflowers, salads, &c." and concluded with pastry, puddings, oranges, and West Indian fruits. Not to overlook libations, James Stuart, Esq.'s glowing description concludes, "The liquids consisted of Champagne, Madeira, sherry, port, claret, porter, lemonade, &c."

Nearly all accounts of Southern cuisine celebrate the plenty of its oceans, forests, skies, and fields. Inhabitants of all classes, including enslaved Africans and sharecroppers, benefited from the fruits and vegetables of the long growing season, the variety of game, and the profusion of fish, mollusks, and things that crawl on the earth, including alligators, turtles, and crawfish. Seaports engaged in international trade provided access to spices, wines and liquors, foodstuffs, and recipes from the British Isles, continental Europe, the Mediterranean, Africa, and the tropics.

The Civil War and decades of turmoil and poverty that followed interrupted trade, upending the South's reputation for sophisticated cuisine, but this did not deter its inhabitants from entertaining graciously, as illustrated in this description of a sparse but congenial dinner party in *Practical Cooking and Dinner Giving: A Treatise Containing Practical Instructions in Cooking; In the Combination and Serving of Dishes; And in the Fashionable Modes of Entertaining at Breakfast, Lunch and Dinner*, published in 1881. "If one has nothing for dinner but soup, hash, and lettuce, put them on the table in style; serve them in three courses, and one will imagine it a much better dinner than if carelessly served."

Many antebellum descriptions of Southern hospitality, particularly those written by outsiders, remark upon the evident role enslaved Africans played in its practice. References to handsomely liveried servants and barefoot children fanning flies with peacock feathers were detailed, often with discomfort and sometimes outright outrage. Without this large enslaved workforce, the linens would not have been so starched and white nor the silver so bright nor the mahogany furniture so richly glowing. Paramount among this domestic labor were the cooks, some sent for training at well-known restaurants and others learning in household kitchens how to cook another race's food with aplomb and creativity.

"To praise the food, and then to say that such dining excellence would not have been possible without slave labor, seems almost to amount to an endorsement of slavery itself," wrote John Edgerton in 1987, in *Southern Food: At Home, on the Road, in History*. "But there is another consideration: To throw out the superlative dishes of the colonial and antebellum periods because of their association with slavery would be to ignore the creative genius of generations of black cooks. . . . The kitchen was one of the few places where their imagination and skill could have free rein and full expression, and there they often excelled. . . . From the elegant breads and meats and sweets of plantation cookery to the inventive genius of Creole cuisine, from beaten biscuits to bouillabaisse, their legacy of culinary excellence is all the more impressive, considering the extremely adverse conditions under which it was compiled."

A GRACIOUS ARCHITECTURE

If the food and drink Southerners provide their guests has a distinctively regional flair, so do the houses in which it's served. Unlike dwellings in colder climates that often have no front appendages at all, save a small roof over the door, a Southern house is rarely without a porch. A social nicety as well as a necessity, the porch creates a wide margin of breeze and shade between indoor and outdoor spaces. There, residents commune with neighbors and passersby, visitors pause and relax, drinks are sipped, meals shared, and after-dinner conversations extend into the balmy night accompanied by concerts of cicadas

and tree frogs. Creating comfort in a hot climate is the guiding principle of traditional Southern house design, but out of this practical consideration grew an exceptionally beautiful architecture. Fine plantation houses acquired dazzling white porticos and colonnades that not only shielded their interiors from direct light but also bestowed a majestic appearance. Modest country homes were endowed with hipped tin roofs that spread out wide and low over wraparound porches, deflecting the sun's heat and glare with halo brightness. Under their exposed brick piers, packed soil cooled the house from below and faithful hounds found a shady place to doze.

Compared to their New England cousins, these houses boast more and bigger windows, higher ceilings, wider halls, and more voluminous central staircases. Triple-sash windows and French doors often open to the porch, forming large indoor/outdoor spaces for living and entertaining. Soaring ceilings invite both heat and voices to rise—these are not rooms for huddling around the fire and conversing in low tones. Wide halls and broad, well-illuminated staircases provide not just passages from here to there but also places to pause and appreciate the beauty of the house and converse with hosts, often with drink in hand. The pace of life in the South before modern air-conditioning was a languorous one and guests were invited to abide awhile, whether on the porch, in the garden, or in airy rooms designed for cross-ventilation. If the hostess's job was to provide every possible comfort her house could afford, the visitor's was to provide conversation and entertainment, including occasional interludes of fiddle music or song.

Dale Couch, scholar of Southern material culture, describes "a sense of welcome that is intrinsic in the design of early Southern houses." This subliminal message starts with the approach to the house, "whether a dirt pathway, an informally lined hedgerow, or grand line of trees and moss aligned with the entry." Clearly visible through a screen of plain porch pillars or statelier white columns, the wide front door stands open, leading to an even wider central hall that often terminates in another open door framing a view of the landscape beyond. "The house is not some looming monolith," says Couch. "There is a progression and a transparency that has an air of hospitality to it." This invitation to approach is reinforced by the porch, an essential part of the progression from public to private space and the first place Southerners offer greetings and gracious gestures to friends and strangers. Buckets of fresh water accompanied by water dippers, plain ones made of dried gourds or fancy ones of coconut shell trimmed with silver, were a common feature. According to Couch, "The etiquette of offering water is not unique to the South, but is characteristic of its hospitality."

PREVIOUS SPREAD: The front porch of the 1825 Bluefields plantation in Mayesville, South Carolina, is built in the style of a "rain porch," with a deep roof supported by freestanding columns that completely shelters the sitting area.

ABOVE: Shaded by live oak trees, this riverfront corner is perfect for large gatherings or quiet conversation. The homeowners host their annual New Year's Eve oyster roast in the fire pit made from antique bricks.

INSIDE THE HOUSE

Whether members of the English or European aristocracy establishing a new branch of the family across the sea or colonial parvenus, wealthy early Southerners were a showy bunch. The houses they built rivaled the Georgian piles and Regency townhouses in vogue back home. They could rarely stow many heirlooms on the small ships they arrived in, so instead they fitted out their houses with the finest things they could import from England, the Continent, and China or beautifully crafted pieces made by skilled local joiners. Until the time of the Civil War, upper-class Southern tastes were on the cutting edge of style, with furniture and other domestic objects valued according to fashion as opposed to sentiment. After the war, however, the opposite was true. A new set of values evolved, one revering the precious things that survived the devastation as vestiges of a former way of life and the ancestors who used them. Atlanta-based interior designer Susan Bozeman talks about how Southern houses today are shaped by this ethos. "When people walk in, they see that you *live* in your house and that it has layers of 'who your family is.' Things in the rooms mean something—they're not just decorative items."

Considering the triple scourges of an uncivil war, the boll weevil, and the Great Depression, it's amazing that anyone had anything at all left by the 1930s. The entire population, whether planter class,

working class, or freed slaves, experienced drastic economic, social, and domestic upheaval. The short story is that people carried on doing the best they could with whatever they had. The longer version is that an attitude was born that no matter how little you had, you shared it generously and with grace. Even though the descendants of planters could no longer afford to pour Madeira into their crystal glasses, they served homemade muscadine wine with equal poise. They didn't apologize if the upholstery was frayed or the paint rubbed thin. Good manners made up for poor circumstances and made everyone feel more at ease than they might have in perfectly polished environs. "Make-do was good," says Alabama-born architect Norman Davenport Askins. "Decorating was less of a fashionable thing and more of an accumulative one, figuring out what to do with the stuff you had."

THE INVITATION

Southern hospitality and the Southern home are entwined—they share the same place and the same spirit. The way we greet and entertain our friends and family is encoded in our architecture and enhanced by our decor. If you've ever entered a Southern house in the midst of a gathering, you know how kindly it receives guests and heightens their sense of camaraderie. If you've ever stepped into an abandoned Southern home, you know how the empty spaces still

resonate with the conviviality of gatherings past and the love shared by family and friends. The houses where this hospitality is practiced can be disarmingly charming or so elegant that it seems they've put on their best party dress to celebrate your coming. The seductive scent of gardenias or magnolia blossoms cut from the yard fills rooms, emanating from heirloom cut-glass vessels or mason-jar vases. Tables are set with fine china or feather-edge pottery arranged on handed-down linens so expertly mended that their imperfections resemble embroidery. Old recipes appear at the table as if conjured from the past—warm biscuits with homemade fig preserves, chicken country captain or hoppin' John, Charlotte Russe or

peach pie. When you sit down at such a table, illuminated by candles or in the shade of a porch, you slip into a timeless reverie where hospitality is the thread that weaves the past to the present and connects each person to the other.

Thank goodness for the rooms—whether dressed in plain beadboard or classical detail—where this zest for life is shared and memories are made that last more than a lifetime. Thank goodness for the people who built and lived in these homes—colonists with big dreams, wives and daughters with ideas and wills of their own, thriving planters and merchants, war widows, struggling farmers, enslaved laborers who gave thanklessly of their skills . . . and to their descendants and the preservationists who have protected these dwellings from harm. Thank goodness for the love of family, joy in friendship, and gladness in meeting strangers that our ancestors possessed and passed onto us. This legacy is an invitation entreating us to join and expand upon the tradition of Southern hospitality, making our homes delightful to guests as well as to ourselves. Charity begins at home, and so does hospitality. It may begin with the impulse to turn our surroundings into comfortable, inspiring places that enhance our own lives, but when we extend that to friends and strangers, we share the most precious gift of all. We invite them into the circle of our lives and shower them with love. The house doesn't need to be perfect. The plates don't have to be expensive or antique. All that really matters is the invitation. Come on in and stay awhile.

First Impressions

FACADES

"They topped the rise and the white house reared its perfect symmetry before her, tall of columns, wide of verandas, flat of roof, beautiful as a woman is beautiful who is so sure of her charm that she can be generous and gracious to all." These are the words with which Margaret Mitchell conveys the first impression of a magnificent plantation house in *Gone with the Wind*. They make vivid the archetypal image of the Southern dwelling—a dazzling white mansion in a rural landscape that manages simultaneously to beckon and impress. From the rolling hills of Virginia to the tidal plains of Georgia and South Carolina and the banks of the Mississippi River, plantation houses rose up in the eighteenth and nineteenth centuries, each expressing its own particular variation of neoclassical idioms—Georgian, Federal, Italianate, and, of course, the South's iconic Greek Revival style. Columns of wood or stone crowned with Doric, Ionic, or Corinthian capitals dressed these edifices with stately porticoes or enwrapped them with colonnades. Pediments and entablatures detailed with modillions and dentil moldings added yet more dignity to these noble facades.

Emulating the great manors of Britain, these houses were intended to inspire awe with their imposing proportions and lavish detail, but they were also designed for comfort. This concession to the demands of living in a hot climate humanized their facades and made them seem less intimidating than the grand mansions they mirrored. "The classical house was re-geared and retrofitted to function in a different atmosphere, with screen doors and louvered shutters that flavor an architecture unlike that of any other region," remarks architect Bobby McAlpine. "These elements animate facades, giving them expression. They also permit the particular dishevelment of Southern houses, the leaning porches and sagging shutters that show life is not still or fixed."

PREVIOUS SPREAD: This new house taps the spirit of the old South with informal wings and large windows and doors. A screen door salvaged from an old river house shelters an entrance that frames a view through the hall to the river beyond.

ABOVE: In the absence of a front porch, ornamental door surrounds can eloquently signal welcome. OPPOSITE: Architect Stan Dixon designed this handsome entrance with a fan-shaped transom and graceful sidelights.

The visual cues of shutters askew and windows flung open invite you to let your hair down, posturing yourself as honestly as the house." Architect Ken Tate sums it up when he describes Southern architecture as gracious rather than "glam." "Southern houses have a human quality that invites emotions into play," he says. "There is an empathy you feel with the beautiful proportions and materials crafted by the human hand."

Not all Southern homes are monumental, but thanks to the necessity of a porch, nearly every house has a row of columns or simple pillars spanning its facade, softening the lines of its architecture the way a smile brightens a face. Although houses in urban streetscapes tend to be private, they still offer signs of welcome and generosity. In Savannah, steps climb high above ground level to front doors and the lavishly ornamented entertaining rooms—but cast-iron balconies overflowing with blooming vines and flowers reach out above the sidewalk to the delight of pedestrians. Charleston single houses turn their narrow sides to face the street, addressing side gardens with their "front" porches. Although this transforms the porch into a private space, wrought-iron gates and fences tangled with Confederate jasmine, wisteria, or roses share the beauty of their gardens with passersby.

LEFT: Architect Ken Tate describes the portico of this Colonial Revival–style house in the Belle Meade neighborhood of Nashville as "a signal of the beauty inside."

In 1850, Swedish author Fredrika Bremer described mid-nineteenth-century Charleston as "a great assemblage of villas standing in their gardens, which are now brilliant with roses of every kind. The fragrance of the orange blossoms fills the air, and the mocking-bird, the nightingale of North America . . . sings in cages in the open windows, or outside them." The scent of fruit trees, the sound of birdsong, and the sight of a hummingbird sipping from honeysuckle flowers in a walled garden prompt the writer to exclaim, "That is something particular, and very beautiful, and I am fortunate to be here"—which is exactly the first impression Southerners want their guests to have.

Bremer described with equal rapture the awe-imposing sight of an oak allée. "The most magnificent . . . of all trees here is the live-oak . . . an immense tree, from the branches of which masses of moss, often three or four yards in length, hung down in heavy draperies." Evoking the image of a lofty Gothic cathedral with arcades and vaulted aisles, she poetically conveys the natural grandeur of such an approach. Whether elevated or humble, tantalizing or direct, the facades of Southern houses and the paths that lead to them convey the same message—"We are happy you're here and glad to share our home with you."

ABOVE: A picket gate and boxwood-lined drive offer a ceremonial approach to this 1813 house in Washington, Georgia. The simple yet commodious double-story porch speaks of leisure and comfort.

OPPOSITE: In Isle of Hope, a historic summering community outside Savannah, Georgia, the deep porches of white-columned houses offer communion with the coastal landscape.

The decorative wrought- and cast-iron gates of Savannah provide street-level interest, even though the front doors are located several steps above the sidewalk. In Charleston, where many of the oldest houses are entered at street level through doors leading to private side porches, overflowing window boxes invite passersby to share in their domestic beauty.

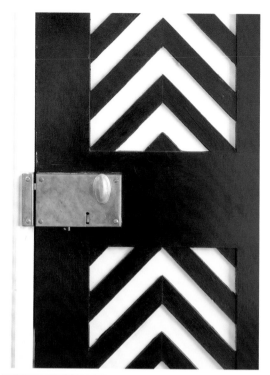

LEFT: A well-decorated door communicates a message that the visitor is not only welcomed but also honored. Lock boxes, decorative painting, elaborate paneling, fine moldings, and brass escutcheons add a sense of ceremony to the moment of entry.

OPPOSITE: Dutch doors with upper panels that open to the breeze and activity of the porch create a sense of relaxed communion between the house and its surroundings. The front door of the Williams family's Colonial Revival house in Savannah, Georgia, is handsomely detailed with sinuous bands of brass.

A Warm Embrace

PORCHES

Conversationalists in the South have a hard time talking without waving their hands, and the region's houses are just as garrulous, gesturing to you broadly before you've even reached the front door. Rare is the house that doesn't greet guests with a porch extending from the facade to gather in friends and family. They can be simple, with squared pillars supporting a corrugated tin roof and a ceiling painted sky blue—a shade that confounds wasps, preventing them from building nests in the upper corners. They can be genteel, with neat rows of white balusters, Victorian jigsaw work, or columns with just a hint of classical style.

And they can be imposing, like the pediment-over-portico entrance of Drayton Hall, near Charleston, with its towering limestone columns and parquet floor. It's hard to imagine relaxing on the latter, but even porches as awe-inspiring as this were occasionally occupied by cigar-smoking gentlemen or ladies flushed from dancing at a ball, fanning themselves in the evening breeze.

In his 1934 novel set in Natchez, Mississippi, *So Red the Rose*, Southern writer Stark Young describes the softer side of classical porches. "Two galleries with fluted columns, one row above the other, ran across the main portion of the house, beyond whose gabled ends were one-storied wings with little columned porches set deep into the garden. The whole air of the house was that of a retreat, a lovely and secret place, strangely formal and domestic at the same time, extravagant but never beyond taste, the product of a romantic feeling and thought." However pretty to look at, porches are practical appendages—semi-enclosed spaces that shade the interior from sun and make it possible to leave windows open when it storms. They were often the coolest place in the house where meals were served, naps taken, and chores like mending, shelling butter beans, or churning ice cream took place. Their style

PREVIOUS SPREAD: Screened doors and windows and louvered shutters are among the many elements that make a Southern house abide in comfort with its surroundings. Although this cottage is new, its spirit and design connect with times of old.

ABOVE AND OPPOSITE: Porch swings and rocking chairs are archetypal images of the Southern way of life—relaxing with family and friends while greeting passersby from the shelter of a jasmine-scented porch.

communicated something about the person who lived in the house, whether planters with an exalted sense of status, modestly successful merchants, or hard-working sharecroppers grateful for the rusty tin roof outside the front door.

Throughout regions of the South, porches take on different forms and names. In Charleston, a porch that traverses the long side of the house to form an open-air living space secluded from the street is called a piazza. In New Orleans, narrow extensions possessing louvered shutters that span the front, sides, or rear facades of buildings are known as galleries. In other parts of the South, wide porches wrapping around the house are called verandas. The term "portico" is used to describe both large formal porches with pediments or entablatures as well as smaller columned entry porches. And often a porch is simply referred to as a porch. Whatever they are called, these spaces form a living bridge between the house and the surrounding landscape, whether that be a green field, a garden, or a cobblestone street. Unlike New England dwellings that button themselves up, Southern houses relax into their surroundings and ask you to do the same. In *Cross Creek*, Floridian novelist Marjorie Kinnan Rawlings describes a long,

LEFT: The design of the piazza of this 1828 plantation-style double house hints at the Barbadian influence on Charleston's architecture. Ideal for the region's semitropical climate, the porch provides a shady, secluded space to converse and catch a breeze.

wide screened veranda as "an invitation to step either inside or out to the yard in lush green grass."

The author captures the liminal nature of porches—places that are not quite inside nor out where we pause before moving back and forth between the protected interior and our unfiltered surroundings. They are semi-sheltered places where we linger alone or with friends, savoring the breeze on our skin. A row of rocking chairs, clusters of wicker furniture including plenty of low tables for drinks, and porch swings all celebrate the pleasures of idling on porches. A capacious portico with towering columns and an elegant portal has an elevating effect, inviting us to stand tall and put on our best manners. A humbler porch with blistering paint and floorboards worn by years of traffic invites us to be comfortable with things as they are. "You can't replicate the patina of wear and tear on an old house," says Jim Strickland, a Georgia-based residential designer specializing in traditional architecture. "Even if the paint's not chipped, it's been scraped— something has happened to it that gives it a life of its own. You can feel the years as you look at it." Whether you converse quietly on a porch or laugh loudly and spill your drink, you become a part of its history, adding a new chapter to its storied past.

OPPOSITE: Primitive Windsor chairs and a simple painted table furnish the porch of this 1850 cottage, a Texas landmark built in the frontier town of Austin by Texas freedom fighter Wayman Wells. Articulated with posts and Italianate cutout balustrades, the porch offers a vernacular expression of classical style.

ABOVE: Homeowners architect Tim Cuppett and garden designer Marco Rini like to serve guests coffee on the front porch using their vintage enameled tin percolator. Cutout balustrades and old wicker furniture set the scene for relaxed Southern hospitality.

OPPOSITE: This back porch is a perfect place to bring the party outside for drinks or dinner on an unexpectedly elegant table surrounded by bistro chairs.

ABOVE: While this claw-foot bathtub accommodates plein-air bathing—bourbon and book in hand—the nursing bench on the front porch of Lee Epting's 1800 farmhouse in Athens, Georgia, is a relic of tender childcare.

ABOVE: Contemporary gilt-rimmed pottery by Jan Burtz, leather-wrapped decanters, and a cake knife designed by Charleston metalsmith Ann Ladson add contemporary style to a front porch tablesetting in Isle of Hope, Georgia.

OPPOSITE: Triple-sash windows connect the indoors with the outdoors, making it easy for guests to join the party on the porch. Homeowner Holley Jaakkola and Paula Danyluk of The Paris Market designed a cyprus-stump table that creates a magical dining destination beneath a rustic chandelier.

In her 1945 book *Favorite Recipes of a Famous Hostess*,
Daisy Breaux, who entertained the
Duke of Windsor before his 1936 abdication,
shares a festive way to enjoy mint juleps.

THE MINT JULEP

"The way I served Mint Julep at the Villa
Marguerita in Charleston became established in the
customs of the South. I had three sizes of silver
bowls—one for a few guests; one for a group of
medium size; and one, a punch bowl, for a large
gathering."

Breaux's recipe calls for completely covering
the bottom of the bowl with tender tops of mint
sprigs, crushed with sugar and water. Add "dry ice,"
that is, finely crushed ice with all the water wrung
out. For six to eight people, pour in a quart of good
whiskey. Completely cover the mixture with a bed
of mint. Provide guests with two straws each—or a
"glass straw"—and invite them to dip into the bowl,
saying:

"Cheek by cheek and
Jaw by jaw,
You sip your julep
Through the straw."

PREVIOUS SPREAD: A modernist addition designed by resident,
architect Alison Spear, can be glimpsed from the traditional setting
of a Charleston piazza furnished with brightly painted chairs
and tables.

ABOVE AND OPPOSITE: Whether served in frosted julep cups or a
repoussé punch bowl, mint juleps are always a welcome treat for
guests gathering on a porch in the steamy Southern twilight.

PREVIOUS SPREAD, LEFT: An easily portable English tilt-top table is ideal for setting an elegant luncheon on the front porch. A mix of coin and sterling silver adds glitter to Old Paris place settings. RIGHT: On a riverside porch near Savannah, Georgia, a Scandinavian bricklayer's palette provides ample space for classic blue-and-white place settings updated with green napkins trimmed in sprightly rickrack.

ABOVE: Tall shutters turn this Savannah, Georgia, porch into a secluded sitting room from which to enjoy the beauty of Forsyth Park's live oak trees. RIGHT: Guests always gravitate toward porch swings where they can sway in the breeze, such as this one in Saint Simons Island, Georgia.

OPPOSITE: Concealed from passersby by a street-front door, the side porches of Charleston single houses, called piazzas, provide an extra room in which to enjoy quiet times with family and friends.

LEFT: Gliders and springy metal chairs are popular furnishings for informal Southern porches. A galvanized-tin watering can filled with colorful flowers completes the laid-back decoration of this country screen porch.

OPPOSITE: Charleston architect David Creech designed this dwelling inspired by West Indian and Southern archetypes. Four pairs of West Indian–style mahogany French doors open to the porch. Classical details include paired columns and pilasters expressed in simple vernacular style.

ABOVE, LEFT: Dark ipe wood floors and a blue ceiling provide cooling visual cues. **RIGHT:** Referencing Thomas Jefferson, Creech refers to his shuttered dining pavilion as the Venetian porch.

RIGHT: French doors with transoms inspired by an eighteenth-century Portuguese villa open to the living room of this Sea Island, Georgia, residence designed by Norman Davenport Askins with Greg Harrell. Retractable screens fitted into the exterior wall turn it into a plein-air gathering space.

ABOVE: A wide porch wraps three sides of this West Indian–style guest cottage on Saint Simons Island, Georgia, designed by John Shackelford. Lattice columns and rafter tails frame the panoramic view. Raised several feet above the ground, the porch becomes an open-air pavilion that seems to float on the marsh.

OPPOSITE: For this porch in Sullivan's Island, South Carolina, architect Beau Clowney drew inspiration from Bermuda and Martinique with the X-shaped design of the railing and upper "walls" of operable shutters.

FOLLOWING SPREAD: Architect Norman Davenport Askins channeled the vernacular architecture of the North Carolina highlands in his use of chestnut-bark shingles and timber posts. Blending into the surrounding woods, the rugged building materials create a sense of comfort and stability.

Come On In

—

ENTRANCE HALLS

People tend to think of halls as passages that lead to rooms where they will spend more time, not rooms themselves where they are encouraged to bide awhile. Below the Mason-Dixon Line, things are different. "In the summertime, people practically lived in their center halls," observes architect Norman Davenport Askins. "Southern halls are deliberately big and historically the coolest place inside the house because they opened from front to back and to the upper floors." A seasonal sitting room, the center hall might also have functioned as a dining room and even a place to sleep, according to nineteenth-century inventories listing beds among their contents. Although it's rare today to discover someone napping in the hall, it's not uncommon to be offered a drink just inside the front door or to dine at tables set up for an overflow of guests. An entertaining area in its own right, the hall is a place where guests may hover for an hour, enjoying cheese straws and conversation without ever even making it to the more conventional entertaining rooms. A perfect location for guests to mingle before heading into the living or dining rooms, it is also the pathway to porches where the party may continue for hours more.

The entrance hall sets the mood for the rest of the house. If it's formal, with ornate neoclassical or Victorian details, guests appreciate the craft that has gone into creating such a beautiful space and feel honored by it. Describing Kenmore, the 1752 home of George Washington's sister, Betty Lewis, architectural historian Virginia Carmichael writes, "In entering the house . . . one is immediately impressed by the large double doorway which leads from the entrance hall to the great room at the rear of the house. The richly carved framework of the door with its fluted pilasters and semi-oval transom adds an unusual touch of dignity and beauty to the whole lower floor." There's no denying that some halls are

PREVIOUS SPREAD: Susan Hable Smith simultaneously enlivens and calms the center hall of her Athens, Georgia, cottage with patterned upholstery from Hable Construction and Neue Galerie wallpaper rendered in monochromatic tones.

ABOVE AND OPPOSITE: Interior designer Athalie Derse chose Farrow & Ball wallpaper as a serene backdrop for furnishings including a Regency bench, George III-style console, and mid-century Maison Jansen chairs for her 1820s Charleston house.

designed to impress. Like their transatlantic antecedents, well-to-do eighteenth- and nineteenth-century Southerners enjoyed a certain amount of pomp and circumstance and the hall was one of the best places to deliver it—particularly in the form of a statuesque staircase. But the architecture of such formal entrance halls need not be seen as boastful or off-putting. Rather, they can be viewed as theatrical stage sets with dramatic, larger-than-life gestures that make guests feel as though they have stepped out of the ordinary into an extraordinary state of being.

Halls that lack such grand detail can be just as enchanting, with subtler enticements like the scent of heart-pine or cypress floorboards and beeswax polish. "The fragrance of an old house says, oh, this is old, this is familiar," observes residential designer Jim Strickland, who often uses reclaimed wood on the floors of center halls for its appearance of age and inimitable fragrance. The painted shiplap walls of a beach cottage hung with black-and-white photos of cherished family gatherings can make a guest feel invited into the intimate life of the house. Paintings, etchings, and photographs made by local artists instantly provide a sense of place. Because it offers both the first and last impression, the entrance hall's decoration should make a statement, but it doesn't

have to be perfect. The entrance hall is one of the places where the furniture definitely doesn't need to match. Sometimes it's the final resting place for inherited pieces that haven't found a place elsewhere in the house because they are either too grand or perhaps a bit eccentric. These are ideally suited for entrance halls. Imperfections like a mismatched pair of chairs flanking an antique console table or fraying silk cushions or candles askew in their sconces convey a sympathetic message—all of us are unique and none of us are perfect.

The first room you enter and the last one you leave, the hall is the alpha and omega of Southern hospitality—and should be paid as much attention to as any other place in the house. This is not only the place where you linger while saying hello; it's also the one where you say good-bye, and Southern farewells are famous for their near interminability. They go on and on, partly because it's rarely too cold to stand by an open door for the ten or twenty minutes they require and partly because it's just so hard to leave. When such feelings of bonhomie have been aroused with the help of fine food, good drink, sparkling conversation, and congenial surroundings, the hall is the ultimate place to savor it before going home.

OPPOSITE: Architect Stan Dixon's design for this Atlanta center hall features the long sweep of a continuous stair rail wrapping around to a landing. Interior designer Susan Bozeman balances the weight of an Empire chest with an English bench and open-based modern console to establish a fresh eclecticism within the formal space.

LEFT: Mississippi-based architect Ken Tate describes the groin vault of this entrance hall as a soft, embracing shape. Furniture selections by Nashville's late interior designer Landy Gardner complement the human scale and subdued elegance of the space.

OPPOSITE: Architect Norman Davenport Askins creates a dramatic focal point in this Federal-style dwelling in Atlanta with full-on period detail, including a pedimented door surround piercing an ornate cornice and delicately articulated moldings. Askins also designed the Chippendale-style consoles that complete the hall's appointments.

OPPOSITE: Furnished with a narrow tailor's table, the center hall of architect Tim Cuppett's primitive farmhouse in Austin, Texas, is large enough to serve as a dining room. In daytime, natural light illuminates the space from all sides and at night, the glossy white paint reflects candlelight shed from a pair of modern iron chandeliers.

LEFT: Pressed and mounted leaves attached to the walls with pushpins provide soft, naturalistic decoration in this plain butted-board hallway. A walnut English chest complements the simple, masculine quality of the space.

RIGHT: A hand-turned hall tree is put to good use at the rear of the hall at Susan Hable Smith's house, where she often dons a garden hat and slip-ons for a quick morning visit to the garden.

OPPOSITE: Smith creates constant visual stimulation in her center hall, where Moroccan brass lanterns, a blue Swedish secretary, a Victorian console, an Art Deco side table, and a modern BDDW credenza share space like an exotic menagerie. For large dinner parties, she clears away much of the furniture and fills the hall with a long trestle table.

OPPOSITE: Regency details including cast-bronze rosettes and wave-shaped moldings contribute rhythmic energy to the continuous sweep of this grand staircase in Atlanta, designed by Norman Davenport Askins.

ABOVE, LEFT: Staircases introduce graceful and sometimes dramatic lines to entrance halls. Architect Stan Dixon echoes the spiral at the base of this stair rail with the sweep of the second-story return. **RIGHT:** The steeply winding rail of this 1869 staircase adds vertical lift to a small entrance hall.

Set a Spell

LIVING ROOMS

The gathering rooms of Southern houses are so varied in size, shape, and decoration, it's hard to believe they belong to the same species. There are majestic Greek Revival double parlors crowned with classical cornices and modest country house sitting rooms with walls of plain plaster or painted plank. The living rooms of Creole plantation houses, with rows of French doors opening to long porches, call to mind the airy architecture of French Colonial and Spanish Colonial villas. Historically, furniture in these rooms was often arranged against the walls and moved as needed to serve a variety of functions from socializing to conducting business to sleeping near the porch doors at night. In the affluent dwellings of the urban South, furniture arrangements were more static, with elegant, rigid-backed chairs and sofas neatly arranged near fireplaces and in cypress-paneled corners.

In Samuel Chamberlain's classic 1956 reference book, *Southern Interiors of Charleston, South Carolina*, the author extols the elegance of high-ceilinged drawing rooms with crystal chandeliers, damask hangings, and mahogany sideboards glistening with family silver as "The hallmark of Charleston, despite the noisy intrusion of this mechanistic century." The pages include many black-and-white photographs of the South's most formal rooms, demonstrating how little styles of decorating changed between the mid-nineteenth and mid-twentieth centuries. While architect Norman Davenport Askins was inspired by the architectural details in the book, he is less enamored of the stiff floor plans, which, he notes, probably date back as far as Federal times in style. "It looks as if there's an alligator pit in the middle of the room or like they're having a wake, sitting around the edges of the room with nobody talking," he observes. Clearly, this is to be avoided.

The most hospitable Southern entertaining rooms deftly combine two messages—that the very

PREVIOUS SPREAD: In Charleston-based designer William Bates's nineteenth-century living room, a woven-grass rug and shagreen-topped table temper the formality of a Georgian Philadelphia camelback sofa.

ABOVE: A capital from an antebellum plantation house serves as a drinks table and display for curiosities. OPPOSITE: The bold lines of an eighteenth-century dressing mirror contrast with a restrained mantel composed by Bates from antique moldings and spalt glass.

OPPOSITE: Georgia-based interior designer Chuck Chewning installed a pair of upholstered screens at one end of his long living room to soften the space and frame a pair of *bronze d'oré* gingko-leaf-inspired lamps from Maison Charles in France. Thanks to their unified palette and similar lines, the traditional upholstery of Italian Louis Seize chairs and a contemporary painting by Carolyn Carr marry harmoniously.

ABOVE: Matching Donghia sofas and glass-and-chrome tables, modern cast-stone mantels, and a pair of eighteenth-century Venetian mirrors unite the parlor's two separate gathering areas into an elegant, eclectic entertaining space.

best has been brought out to welcome the guest and that the guest is invited to relax. "Inviting people into immediate comfort is an essential part of Southern hospitality," says architect Bobby McAlpine. "You need chairs, tables by the chairs, and all the props. What they look like doesn't matter as much as the fact that you have made a place for someone who might visit." Architect Ken Tate considers a handsome fireplace an essential feature in any Southern living room, not just for warmth but also because it establishes a hearth and a feeling of home, of sitting around the fire with the dog. "A beautiful mantel is critical," he adds. "There are no two ways about it—if it's a traditional Southern house, the mantel has to be classical." Lighting was also important in traditional Southern drawing rooms, as illustrated by eighteenth- and nineteenth-century inventories listing chandeliers, mirrored wall sconces, candelabra, candlesticks, and candle stands. Contemporary hosts and hostesses are wise to consider just as many light sources, both natural and artificial, because, as Askins says, "Nobody looks good in canned light."

Fine heirlooms or charming country antiques may be what first comes to mind when imagining a Southern sitting room, but the age and style of the furniture is less important than the spirit of the room.

RIGHT: Sunlight bathes the high-ceilinged living room of designer Holley Jaakkola's Isle of Hope home near Savannah, Georgia. White walls, mirrored panels, and off-white slipcovers intensify the bright, airy atmosphere of the room where her daughters and friends often share an hour of music.

According to interior designer Susan Bozeman, the best rooms are not "set up." They should clearly be intended for people to come in and enjoy themselves. She advocates filling rooms with collections and things that tell stories about the people who live there, like the butter churn she inherited from her grandmother that inspired a collection of Southern crocks in her living room. Most Southern gathering rooms feature tabletops or corner cupboards where treasured objects are arranged—blue-and-white Canton china that was brought over by the barrelful in British trading ships, hand-painted portrait miniatures and framed silhouettes, travel souvenirs collected by the residents or their ancestors, a saucer filled with hand-wrought nails from the old home place. When the room is filled with people, these compositions spark storytelling. When it's empty, it seems quite plausible that they talk among themselves.

All of these elements combine to create rooms that are irresistibly inviting. "When you inventory your friends, one of them has the house you want to go to more than others," says McAlpine. "They've tapped something that makes you feel more the way you want to feel. There's something about it that's true. That's the house you want to go to."

PREVIOUS SPREAD: Black paint transforms the beadboard walls of architect Tim Cuppett's living room into a modern backdrop for furniture and art spanning two centuries.

LEFT: Peggy Galis displays inherited furniture, decorative objects, baskets, and pottery with an artistic eye in her Athens, Georgia, home.

OPPOSITE: Peggy Galis assembles heirlooms including a hand-carved decoy, a matriarchal photo-portrait, and a stone from the chimney of Meriwether Lewis's boyhood home in a conversational corner where stories practically tell themselves.

ABOVE: A panoply of baskets, decoys, Chinese jars, and memorabilia are arranged in compelling compositions throughout the two living rooms of Galis's 1840 Athens, Georgia, house.

RIGHT AND OPPOSITE: Atlanta-based interior designer Susan Bozeman introduces a contemporary blue and ivory palette to the formal living room of this neotraditional home designed by architect Stan Dixon. While the mantelpiece displays intricate Federal-style detail, the remaining architecture of the room is expressed in a restrained voice that skews both modern and traditional. While ornamental *girondelles* echo the mantel's decorative elegance, for the most part, the furnishings possess classic modern lines.

ABOVE: Many in the South consider cheese straws served in silver or cut-glass bowls de rigueur for entertaining. A word to the wise: if you don't have time to make them, lie.

OPPOSITE: Margie Spalding's Athens, Georgia, living room features an antique chinoiserie bamboo coffee table with a panel of hand-painted silk wallpaper under glass. A nineteenth-century claret jug with sherry glasses repurposed for martinis promises enlivening libations.

Dodgie Shaffer of Montgomery, Alabama, owner of Zelda Fitzgerald's copy of *Joy of Cooking*, spoke candidly with Scott Peacock about this Southern classic for *The Alabama Project*.

CHEESE STRAWS: AN HONEST OPINION

This would be heresy to almost anybody I know to hear me say what would be my true, deep, heartfelt feelings about cheese straws. In my opinion, cheese straws are vastly overrated. They are, of course, an institution in the South. You can't have a wedding, you can't have a funeral, you can't have a gift, you can't have anything without cheese straws. I can. I have made cheese straws. It's not worth the effort in my opinion. I don't know where cheese straws came from. Where did they come from? I think it's one of those things like the boll weevil that they brought in and it just spread all over.

The Classic Recipe
adapted from *Charleston Receipts*, 1950

1 pound sharp Cheddar cheese, grated
¼ pound butter, room temperature
½ teaspoon salt
¼ teaspoon cayenne pepper
1¾ cups flour

Preheat the oven to 350°F.

In a medium bowl, cream the butter and cheese. Add the salt and cayenne. Then add the flour.

Pack the dough in a cookie press and pipe ribbons, or roll the dough thin and cut it into narrow strips, 4 inches long. Place on a greased cookie sheet about an inch apart. Bake for 25 minutes, or until golden. Makes about one hundred straws.

ABOVE AND OPPOSITE: Defining the appeal of decorative Federal-style moldings, architect Ken Tate quotes Diana Vreeland: "The eye has to travel." Even if waiting for their hostess or other friends, guests are actively engaged by the architecture and furnishings selected both for comfort and visual stimulation by late Nashville interior designer Landy Gardner. An arcaded dining hall joins the living and dining rooms, creating a circulation place during cocktail parties and an additional seating area for dinner.

OPPOSITE: Family portraits and an eclectic array of chairs populate the double parlor that serves as artist Susan Hable Smith's formal dining and living rooms.

ABOVE: Smith is not afraid of color or pattern, as illustrated in these rooms where pink takes center stage. "No one ever is grouchy in a pink room and everyone looks good," she says. A pair of Empire-style couches with fringe upholstery, contemporary art, op art wallpaper, and a tole chandelier create a fanciful tableau. Linen curtains with wooden tiebacks and a simple Danish table downplay the theatrical decor.

LEFT TO RIGHT: Architect and interior designer Alison Spear decorated her Charleston house with a combination of family pieces, new finds, and modern decor. While the corner cabinet, oil portrait, and Aubusson carpet might have translated into stuffy, traditional decor, chartreuse walls and moldings update the look. African-inspired side tables that double as stools, designed by modern masters Charles and Ray Eames, and amply upholstered furniture make this small living room an inviting spot for gatherings.

RIGHT: Interior designer Susan Bozeman combined the homeowner's collections of creamware and black papier-mâché trays in dynamic compositions. Wood, metal, gilded leather, and creamware create a visually engaging vignette in the living room.

OPPOSITE: Trays with straight and fluted edges, a duo of diminutive bull's-eye mirrors, and a Federal console table form a focal point at the end of an axis.

Dinner Is Served

DINING ROOMS

In modern life, the dining room tends to be the most underutilized space in the house. Family meals are taken in the kitchen or breakfast room or on trays in the room with the biggest TV. Dinners for friends tend to be just as casually served, without the ceremony associated with the formal dining room, where table and sideboard and ranks of chairs seem to assume stiff postures of boredom. But in the realm of Southern hospitality, the importance of this room is rivaled only by that of the porch. Replete with candles, flowers, silver and crystal vessels, and offerings of food and libations, it is a temple to the domestic arts and a sanctuary reserved for conviviality. It is also a place to commune with the past and bring it forward, employing heirloom silver and china that carry memories of the people who used it before. "These things have emotional resonance," says Dawn Corley, one of the South's best-known silver experts.

According to Corley, silver is a symbol of welcome and the signal of a civilized environment. Gently correcting those who feel that setting the table with silver creates too formal a tone, she observes, "Silver is a symbol of leisure—when you're around it, you're allowed to relax and enjoy it. You know you don't have to hurry." Great pleasure can be found in bedecking the table, raiding the silver chest, linen closet, and cabinets where china, crystal, and cut glass is stored. Rarely seen things are brought out into the light of day, as described in this passage from Josephine Pinckney's 1945 novel, *Three O'Clock Dinner*, set in Charleston: "The big gold and white Sevres epergne had come down from the garret whither it went in summer when windows were open and rude winds blew; with its load of white gladioli and long trails of asparagus fern it gave a monumental festiveness to the table. Banished was the blue Canton china of every day and the company set filled each place with a pool of beflowered green porcelain.

PREVIOUS SPREAD: Alison Spear sets an eclectic table with heirloom Art Deco napkins and eighteenth-century French faience plates. OPPOSITE: Spear created a calm mood in the dining room with pale blue paint, enlivening it with a melange that includes antique American and English furniture, an African rug, and a Venetian chandelier. set an eclectic table.

ABOVE: An early twentieth-century *verre eglomisé* panel dresses up the swinging door that opens from Spear's dining room to the kitchen.

The empty glasses like little lamps held up sparkles of light."

Suggestions from Mary Henderson's 1881 guide to entertaining, *Practical Cooking and Dinner Giving*, include specific ideas about setting the table. "It is as pleasant a change to see an individuality or a characteristic taste displayed in the setting of the table and the choice of dishes as in the appointments of our houses or in matters of toilet. At different seasons the tables might be changed to wear a more appropriate garb. It may be solid, rich, and showy, or simple, light, and fresh. . . . By far the most elegant arrangement consists in having different sets of plates, each set of a different pattern, for every course. Here is an unlimited field for exquisite taste."

The decoration of the dining room itself also provides opportunities for ravishing the guest with beauty. "You need to create something that makes people want to be there and to stay a long time," says interior designer Jackye Lanham. "It's a place where you can add drama, having deep rich colors, or putting fabric on the walls. These things encompass you acoustically and visually so you feel embraced in the space." Dining rooms are also favorite settings for scenic wallpaper, including the intricate woodblock prints produced in the late nineteenth century by

LEFT: Within the sunny Southern atmosphere of artist Susan Hable Smith's dining room, the worn velvet of French chairs, an Argentine marble-topped table, and *bronze-d'oré* candelabras inject continental European style. A Hable Construction wool rug and French bubble-glass chandelier add modern voices into the mix.

Zuber, de Gournay, and Joseph Dufour. The latter's Monuments of Paris design is particularly popular in the South, perhaps because George and Martha Washington chose it for their Mount Vernon dining room (Napoleon and Joséphine Bonaparte used it first at Fontainebleau). Wrapping the room with fanciful images of architecture, natural wonders, and botanical curiosities, scenic wallpaper and murals add a touch of the exotic and deepen the sense of intimacy guests feel gathering around the candles in the center of the room.

Dining rooms can be the most beautiful space in the house—and yet not enough hours of the day are enjoyed there. Architect Bobby McAlpine suggests that they be tasked with multiple functions, such as libraries, or placed in highly trafficked areas within the house. "Wooden dining tables have the capacity to hold memory," he says. "More than just waiting for a party, they should gain knowledge, history, and experience. Dining tables should be touched and seen and put to work. It's not good to keep them waiting." Let this be an exhortation to Southern hosts and hostesses who are neglecting their dining tables, as well as all the glittering accoutrements associated with them. Don't reserve the dining room for rare occasions. Don't let the dust rag be the only thing that touches your table. Treat yourself and your family as generously as you do your guests. Hospitality begins at home.

ABOVE: A mix of contemporary table- and glassware with ornate, antique silver candlesticks and a pretty floral centerpiece combines the formal with the informal, turning even the most relaxed meal into a special event.

OPPOSITE: Graceful carved chair backs and a banquette tucked into the bay window add appeal to a sun-drenched alcove that serves as both breakfast room and informal dining area. Generous floor-to-ceiling curtains soften the area visually and acoustically.

LEFT: To create spaces that are simultaneously sumptuous and relaxing, interior designer Chuck Chewning often combines the high with the low and the new with the old. In this spirit, he married a pair of nineteenth-century crystal candelabra with West Elm chrome-and-glass consoles and Italian gilt-wood mirrors in his Savannah dining room.

OPPOSITE: Chewning chose a contemporary painting by Atlanta artist Carolyn Carr to contrast with the set of classical American chairs that surround his formal dining table. A rotating array of china sets the tables for dinner parties, including this gilt-rimmed Richard Ginori Fiesole pattern, hand painted with bucolic scenes of Italy.

OPPOSITE AND LEFT: Southerners have long favored mural wallpaper for their dining rooms, emulating their English- and French-style mentors. This English picturesque-style house in Marietta, Georgia, still features its original early twentieth-century grisaille wallpaper, thanks in part to the restoration work of artist Jill Biskin from Athens, Georgia. For an understated modern accent, interior designer Susan Bozeman combined comfortable contemporary upholstered dining chairs with George III-style chairs and introduced red into the palette.

ABOVE: The dining room is a perfect place for warm colors and extravagant touches, like this red silk wall covering chosen by interior designer Jackye Lanham. Trim in a deeper shade of red accentuates the beauty of intricate moldings.

OPPOSITE: Designed by architect Norman Davenport Askins, the dining room of this Federal-style house includes an arched exedra accommodating a custom-designed serving table.

Chef Stephanie Tyson's recipe for flash-pickled green tomatoes from *Well Shut My Mouth!: The Sweet Potatoes Restaurant Cookbook* offers a fresh alternative to watermelon pickle, and her tomato jam recipe, from *Soul Food Odyssey*, jazzes up Sunday roasts and sandwiches.

GREEN TOMATO CARPACCIO

¼ cup cider vinegar
2 tablespoons sugar
1 tablespoon pickling spice
1 pound green tomatoes, thinly sliced

In a nonreactive saucepan, combine the vinegar, sugar, and pickling spice and heat for about 5 minutes, or until the sugar dissolves. Pour the mixture over the green tomatoes and marinate for at least an hour.

QUICK TOMATO JAM

4 cups canned diced tomatoes
½ cup balsamic vinegar
1 cup sugar
1 teaspoon dried tarragon
2 teaspoons chopped garlic
¼ teaspoon crushed red pepper flakes
1 teaspoon dried thyme
1 teaspoon salt

Combine all the ingredients in a medium-size saucepan. Simmer for about 30 minutes, or until the mixture reaches a jam-like consistency. Refrigerate before serving.

OPPOSITE AND RIGHT: "Formal felt everyday for some Southerners," says architect Ken Tate, who grew up in the Greek Revival grandeur of Columbus, Mississippi. For a Colonial Revival–inspired dwelling in the Belle Meade neighborhood of Nashville, Tennessee, he designed a Georgian dining room with a swan pediment overmantel and arched recessed cabinets for the homeowner's collection of antique china. Although its architectural detail is dramatic, the room's monochrome palette allows attention to focus upon conversation around the table.

LEFT: Walls provide an oft over-looked opportunity for displaying inherited china, as seen here in the dining room of Peggy Galis, where gilt-rimmed plates share space with twentieth-century arrow-shaped sconces and a historical painting by contemporary artist Jill Biskin. Rock-crystal candelabras and an English silver tea set stand atop the flame-mahogany sideboard.

OPPOSITE: A neoclassical side-board holds fine silver on its top surface and shelters rustic baskets and pottery below—all bounty from ancestral properties. The arrow-shaped sconces provide the perfect complement to a collection of nine-teenth-century Thomas McKenney and James Hall lithographs of Native American chieftains.

PREVIOUS SPREAD: New Orleanian Peter Patout dressed up his French Quarter dinner table and bar with heirloom French china, crystal, and silver, as well as Bohemian-glass decanters and an Old Paris epergne.

ABOVE AND OPPOSITE: Cotton bolls decorate the table at Bluefields, the plantation home of fourth-generation resident Ashleigh Goza. Spindle-back chairs surround a long table covered with a canvas drop cloth. Polished silver and gilt-rimmed china share the tabletop with woven-grass placemats and napkin rings. Bouquets of turkey feathers and a nineteenth-century print of a quail attest to the area's bountiful game.

OPPOSITE AND ABOVE: Garden and floral designer Holley Jaakkola brings the outside into her dining room, with lichen-green paint and decoration drawn from nature. Wildflowers in simple glass containers garnish the table. Garden cloches on the sideboard cover plates, shells, and ferns cut from the garden. On the mantel, silver, mercury glass, feathers, horn, and ceramic mushrooms complement an arrangement of ornithological prints and modern art.

RIGHT AND OPPOSITE: Interior designers Carter Kay and Nancy Hooff conjure a glamorous mood in the dining room of a Tudoresque cottage in Atlanta, Georgia. Furnishings including Louis Quinze–style chairs, a marble-top console, and an eighteenth-century Italian credenza add Old World elegance, as do wooden columns with polychrome shafts and gilded capitals. In the room's center, a contemporary glass-and-acrylic table appears to float above an Oushak carpet with a cloudlike palette of pale blue, cream, and gold.

OPPOSITE: American interior design icon Billy Baldwin would have approved of the dark brown shade William Bates employed in the dining room of his 1829 Charleston single house. The pairing of a vintage Danish-modern table set with family china and crystal and a French *bronze-d'oré* and rock-crystal chandelier is equally timeless in style. Arsenic-tinted glass and bronze tiebacks, circa 1840, add more jewelry to the room.

LEFT: Chairman of architecture at the American College of the Building Arts, Bates possesses twin passions for the old and the new. The sleek console table he designed with a blind frieze and fluted Doric legs offers a case in point.

RIGHT: A tropical mural inspired by late eighteenth-century woodblock wallpaper and a simple pine floor disguised as parquet inject lighthearted elegance to the dining room of a South Carolina beach house designed by architect Beau Clowney. Interior designer Jenny Keenan deftly combines rattan butterfly thrones, leather upholstered chairs, and a pecky-cypress tabletop on a vintage McGuire base.

OPPOSITE: Keenan brings this same love of diverse style and material to another coastal dining room, this time marrying walnut, cypress root, glass, and rope. Well versed in Southern vernacular architecture, Clowney employs tall sash windows that open into wall pockets to maximize exposure to cooling sea breezes.

OPPOSITE: Decorated with leaves plucked from a flowering grape vine, a silver fox, and china painted with a grape motif, this tea table setting recalls a favorite Aesop's fable. With sterling silver and horn-handled flatware, a crystal decanter etched with grape leaves, and a hand-embroidered tea cloth, this arrangement features just a fraction of silver expert Dawn Corley's collection of tableware.

ABOVE, LEFT: The subject of seafood always brings out whimsy in the design of tableware. Consider, for example, this hand-painted oyster plate, complete with a shell-shaped sauceboat, that mimics the lavender iridescence of oyster shells, an ornate triton-shaped spear, and chinoiserie oyster forks, circa 1870, decorated with bamboo-style handles and naturalistic animals. **RIGHT:** English Blind Earl china, collected by New Orleanian Quinn Peeper, features a colorful raised pattern.

Dawn Corley, a highly respected silver expert known as "The Charleston Silver Lady," offers some surprising thoughts about silver care.

SILVER CARE

It doesn't bother me if my silver doesn't gleam. I actually prefer it with a soft sheen. But I also don't mind polishing it occasionally. It's a way of meditating on the memories that each piece holds. If you put white chalk inside a vessel or tea set, it absorbs sulfur and deters pitting.

In the South, you must never store silver in plastic or newspaper, because this accelerates pitting. Wrap infrequently used pieces in white muslin or cotton diapers, then roll them in anti-tarnish silver cloth.

I never put flatware in the dishwasher, where it is sealed in a hot, acidic environment. Instead, I polish flatware with white toothpaste, leaving it on for a few minutes before rinsing with hot water. This leaves your silver clean and free of chemical residue.

LEFT TO RIGHT: According to Corley, pearl-handled forks are ideally suited for dessert courses and summer dining. A crystal "spooner" holds a stash of forks for guests to collect while circumnavigating a table abounding in cakes, pies, and punch. While a Bailey, Banks & Biddle single-serving teapot takes on the form of a Grecian urn, a rare silver basket and eighteenth-century Spanish Colonial teaspoons emulate the gossamer texture of hand-crocheted lace.

Pretty Privies

POWDER ROOMS

Until recent times, nicely decorated indoor powder rooms were a rarity in Southern houses. A visit to the necessary conveniences used to require a five-hundred-foot trot to the privy outside. At Monticello, Thomas Jefferson, a pioneer of "modern" household technology, did his best to make the experience a pleasant one, designing two state-of-the-art privies nearer the house featuring Venetian blinds and pyramidal roofs with ball finials. He also configured three small indoor privies whose proximity to entertaining and sleeping rooms made up for their cramped dimensions. Although in use much earlier in Paris and London, indoor hydraulic plumbing didn't become widely available in America until the mid-nineteenth century and was considered as much a status symbol as a sought-after convenience. English architect William Jay, designer of several of Savannah's most impressive early nineteenth-century dwellings, brought with him this technological know-how, a fact that undoubtedly enhanced his reputation.

Before flush toilets became common, however, affluent hosts did what they could to provide their guests a pleasant indoor experience, furnishing small paneled rooms with chamber pots by Minton, Royal Doulton, Spode, and Wedgwood, often in the blue-and-white palette favored by the English and Southerner alike. These tiny chambers would also have included ewers and water basins of similarly luxurious design and starched linen towels. When old Southern houses were first upgraded to incorporate indoor plumbing, the stylistic results were rarely attractive. The fixtures were ugly and the bathrooms were shoehorned under staircases or relegated to rickety additions at the rear of the house. As a rule, the powder room was, in the words of interior designer Jackye Lanham, "a gloomy, lonely, cold interior space with no windows." This is a far cry from the powder rooms of today, where

PREVIOUS SPREAD: Highly figured Brunschwig & Fils wallpaper, glossy paint, and a collection of eye portraits give this powder room a surprising look.

ABOVE AND OPPOSITE: New finger towels indistinguishable from heirloom ones hail from the Horseshoe Crab, Savannah's go-to destination for embroidered linens. Chinoiserie wallpaper, a baroque mirror, and rock-crystal and *bronze-d'oré* sconces introduce touches of Georgian grandeur to this diminutive space.

homeowners and designers embark on flights of fancy to create jewel-box spaces with opulent fixtures and elegant decor.

"The powder room is a place where you can use your imagination," says New Orleans–based interior designer Rosemary James. "You can take a small space and make it seem larger by using decorative treatments—painted stripes or architectural murals. You can let it be any kind of room you want." Painter and muralist Jill Biskin, a former set painter for the New York Metropolitan Opera, enjoys creating architectural illusions and fanciful designs within the small scale of the powder room. "I want guests to close the door and be alone in a special little room. By virtue of being so close to the walls, they can meditate on the details—it's a one-on-one experience." Biskin's designs range from simple stripes that visually enlarge the space to botanical and architectural murals and shimmering gold-leafed walls and ceilings.

Lanham observes that the powder room provides an opportunity to add a little sparkle or unexpected glamour to the house. "It's a great place to display small art or special treasures that make it more interesting," she says, like the collection of silver card cases she mounted on a powder room's walls. James, whose husband owns New Orleans's Faulkner House Books, lined a powder room with beautifully bound volumes, transforming it into a Lilliputian library. Silver expert Dawn Corley shares her love of silver with guests, using a highly polished silver dower tray as the mirror above the lavatory and adding more glitter with smaller trays and powder jars.

While some might consider books or silver optional, most Southern hosts and hostesses agree that linen towels are required as a way of showing guests you value them. Since powder rooms don't get that much use, ironing the towels isn't too much of a burden considering the pleasure they give. Nor is taking the time to arrange a little nosegay from whatever's blooming in the garden or light a scented candle or set out colognes or old-fashioned toilet water that is a welcome treat for guests in a hot climate. A thoughtfully prepared powder room is more than a convenience—it is an unexpected gift. When guests open the door and find something beautiful and thoughtful inside, they know their host or hostess has taken an extra step to do something special for them.

OPPOSITE: Interior designer Susan Bozeman chose Lewis & Wood's Bacchus wallpaper with an oversized foliated pattern to make a dramatic statement in this Atlanta powder room. Finding inspiration in the swanky fixtures of early twentieth-century bathrooms in New York hotels, she selected Art Deco–style wall lights and a Venetian Art Deco mirror.

RIGHT: Artist Jill Biskin created a shimmering palladium ceiling and moon-gold wall treatments to reflect soft light from early twentieth-century sconces in this Palmetto Bluff, South Carolina, home.

OPPOSITE: A tiny bronze chandelier, gilt-framed mirror, and marble lavatory lend touches of elegance to the plain board walls of this coastal cottage powder room.

Stay Awhile

GUEST ROOMS

Like every region, even the South has a quantity of cluttered, make-shift guest bedrooms. But it also has more than its fair share of sunny, airy spare rooms with four-poster beds, white crocheted canopies, and an array of heirloom furnishings, faintly fragranced with the scent of beeswax. In less formal settings on the coast or in the mountains, you might find colorful chenille bedspreads, brightly painted furniture, rag rugs or hooked ones, and bouquets of daisies or dahlias cut from the yard. While style is a matter of taste, etiquette demands that the room be a tangible expression of the host's gladness to see his or her guests and desire for them to feel not simply comfortable, but also cherished. This message is encoded into the decoration of the best Southern guest rooms, where personal touches like family antiques or creatively displayed collections combine with simple necessities, such as space in the closet, and little luxuries that may not be enjoyed in everyday living.

In the old South, people traveled long distances to visit family, friends, or business associates, so guest rooms were an important part of every affluent household. Whether a room reserved for the purpose or a personal bedroom temporarily restyled for visitors, every effort was made to ensure that it provided all a guest might need while visiting. Interior designer Jackye Lanham refers to the guest room as the Queen's Room, hearkening back to the days when Queen Elizabeth I toured her kingdom, nearly bankrupting hosts who turned their houses upside down and inside out to honor their monarch. "You should have the best of everything in the guest room," she says. "Beautiful decoration, wonderful linens, candles and other fragranced things, sewing kits and toothbrushes, and anything else that might be forgotten."

In *Mrs. Whaley Entertains: Advice, Opinions, and 100 Recipes from a Charleston Kitchen*, published in 1998, Emily Whaley declares, "There should be

PREVIOUS SPREAD AND ABOVE: Despite an energizing palette of red, orange, and hot pink, this guesthouse bedroom designed by Alison Spear has a restful, atmosphere. The barrel-vaulted ceiling arcs down low toward the window's brow creating a cozy alcove.

OPPOSITE: Vintage furniture tucked beneath the slanted ceilings of this attic-floor bedroom invites a good night's rest. Flowered chintz curtains, cotton quilts, and an embroidered Indian rug combine in a soothing color scheme of pink and green.

a touch of luxury. . . . Two or three rosebuds make a hit in the bedrooms. New magazines to idle with. There should be new, inspiring, and much talked of books within reach. . . . Every bedroom should have a vacuum pitcher of ice water and glasses and napkins, and the beds should be obviously luxurious looking. Small soft pillows, colorful throws to snuggle under for a short nap. In the bathroom a cake or so of Yardley's English Lavender and a fresh box of Kleenex."

The typical furnishings of guest rooms in traditional Southern homes vary from complete sets of the weighty Second Empire furniture favored in the Victorian age to the more graceful rice bed, so named for its posts carved with depictions of rice plants. Most Southern guest bedrooms feature an array of pieces handed down through various lines of the host's family. Delicate objects such as candle stands and sewing boxes that might be overlooked in larger, more public rooms make perfect guest room furnishings. So do the embroidered dresser scarves and crocheted antimacassars brought out from hiding in cedar chests and placed under lamps and vases. It's not possible to get too charming or old-fashioned in the guest bedroom, which should be a place where

LEFT: The sepia-toned painting of a low country marsh by Savannah artist Bob Christian sets the dreamy mood of this guest room on the fourth floor of a nineteenth-century Italianate house in Savannah, Georgia. Brown-and-white toile complements the soft tone of the marble mantelpiece's veining.

RIGHT: The mid-nineteenth-century guest cottage behind Marion Slaton's house in Washington, Georgia, was originally a cook's house and kitchen. With far less ornate interior architecture than the primary residence, it features simple butted-board wainscoting and plain door surrounds.

OPPOSITE: Toile detailed with pastoral scenes covers the walls of a bedroom decorated with simple English and American antiques and an early Audubon elephant portfolio print. Together, the contents of the room convey the sense of a country getaway appropriate to the rural, agricultural location.

visitors enjoy a temporary respite from the stress and demands of everyday life.

No Southern guest room is complete without a touch of silver, painted china, or cut glass. These rooms provide the perfect opportunity to take little-used family heirlooms out and locate them in plain sight. Placing valued objects within easy reach of guests is a way of pampering them. Silver expert Dawn Corley arranges silver-topped powder jars filled with cotton balls and toiletries on the dresser so guests don't need to rummage around in drawers to find what they need. She also places a large silver gallery tray on the bed to hold local magazines, tea bags and water, and silver bowls filled with candies and cookies. "Antique silver carries a message of love, even if it didn't belong to your family," she observes. "It sets a tone." This feeling of being warmly embraced by friends, as if you were family— or by family, as if you were a beloved friend—is the essence of Southern hospitality at home.

RIGHT: This bedroom designed by Athalie Derse appears more cosmopolitan than Southern in style, despite the fact that it is found in a dwelling in Charleston, South Carolina. Transatlantic furnishings, including a monumental English neoclassical tester bed and period Gustavian klismos chairs, combine with a modern mirrored chest that introduces a chic mid century detail.

OPPOSITE: A red-and-cream palette and family antiques make this gabled guest room a cozy retreat.

ABOVE, LEFT: Walls of irregularly sized pine boards covered with blue milk paint and a hand-turned four-poster bed with a vintage fringed bedspread endow this guest room in an 1800 farmhouse with country charm. RIGHT: Designed by architect Jim Strickland to resemble the interior of an old chinked-log house, this bedroom offers a warm, rustic atmosphere.

RIGHT: Designer William Bates furnished a small bedroom with exaggerated gestures, including a mahogany Empire bed from Boston, a Florentine gilt mirror, architectural prints, an armchair with vermiculated velvet upholstery, and tables he designed with a Greek key motif.

OPPOSITE: An Old Paris urn filled with flowers adds an antique touch to a bathroom with 1920s style.

ABOVE, LEFT: A bathroom with plank walls, a painted claw-foot tub, and handmade stool captures the country character of this old Texas farmhouse.

RIGHT: In designer Holley Jaakkola's guesthouse bathroom, an elaborate eighteenth-century Italian basin provides Old World counterpoint to modern marble tile walls.

ABOVE: Dawn Corley pampers guests with a silver tray laden with homemade candies, tea, and flowers.

OPPOSITE: Mounted horns of exotic game and a stack of vintage suitcases contribute to the spirit of Southern eccentricity that characterizes this plantation-house guest room.

Dawn Corley, "The Charleston Silver Lady," suggests placing this sweet bedtime truffle on a silver plate in the guest room at night.

MARTHA WASHINGTON CANDY

This indulgent candy has been made in my family for as long as I can recall. Because it is made of just a few simple ingredients, each must be the best you can buy. And contrary to what you've been told, salted butter is the way to go. This recipe is adapted from an old one, handwritten by my great-grandmother and dated 1919.

8 cups confectioners' sugar, sifted 5 times
¾ cup (3 sticks) salted butter, at room temperature
5 tablespoons clear vanilla extract or orange extract
4 boxes dark Baker's unsweetened chocolate
A few curls paraffin
2 cups pecan halves

Mix the sugar, butter, and vanilla or orange extract until smooth. Take a small amount in your hand and roll it into a log the shape and size of a Tootsie Roll. Set onto waxed paper and place in the refrigerator until firm and very cold.

In a small saucepan, melt the chocolate and paraffin until blended to a glossy sheen. Working quickly, dip each chilled candy into the chocolate. Once coated, allow the excess chocolate to drip off, then place the candy on wax paper and immediately press a pecan half into the top. Store airtight in the refrigerator.

The Heart of the House

KITCHENS

"A table for communion and a pantry with a bag of good stone-ground grits is my idea of a Southern kitchen," says Lee Epting, an Athens, Georgia–based caterer and preservationist. Epting has rescued several endangered houses and arranged them in a place called The Hill, where he lives and hosts entertainments, intimate and grand. "I also require a bar with good bourbon, a fireplace full of iron Dutch ovens, and more iron cookware to add warmth and ambiance." His kitchen at The Hill features a five-foot-wide fireplace with a bread oven and iron cranes to hold heavy pots above the fire and a good-sized table with a cool marble top for making bread and biscuits and serving buffet-style meals. These things hearken back to the days when kitchens were utilitarian in design—skin-scorching, downright dangerous spots built a safe distance away from the main house. But even in those days, they were also gathering places where those who worked found time for conversation and a hot-off-the-stove snack as they baked, boiled, and roasted meals for their employers.

Southern housewives in the early days of modern kitchen design had their own modest share of discomfort. According to Matt Lee, co-author of *The Lee Bros. Charleston Kitchen*, published in 2013, "a classic Charleston kitchen was a terrible place for most of the twentieth century." Usually tacked to the back of the house in an awkward addition, it had next to no cupboard or counter space and rarely more than a hot plate or miniscule stove for cooking. "How dreadful your kitchen was became almost a point of pride—a touchstone to the deprivations of the Depression and the early twentieth-century post–Civil War days," he says. Jim Strickland, whose designs for Southern houses frequently feature rooms where cooking and entertaining happen simultaneously, points out that early to mid-twentieth-century kitchens were lonely places. "Now, very few people

PREVIOUS SPREAD: A French Lacanche stove and antique stone containers inject Old World charm into this Southern kitchen.

ABOVE AND OPPOSITE: Contemporary gilt-rimmed pottery by Jan Burtz and hand-forged flatware by Charleston artisan Ann Ladson lend a touch of craft to a kitchen table designed by homeowner Holley Jaakkola and fashioned by Sabenati Custom Designs.

go alone into one room and cook a huge meal while everybody else gathers somewhere," he remarks. "We're all so busy, we don't want to lose the opportunity to talk to each other, even if we're doing something that in the past was considered a chore."

Once modern kitchens grew large enough to hold a few people, they tended to fill up beyond capacity during parties. Southern hosts and hostesses had to develop strategies to keep the entire party from migrating there, such as putting all the food and drink at the opposite end of the house. Still, the party came. That's why most Southerners put out finger food like Virginia peanuts, cream cheese with pepper jelly, or pickled okra on the counter or breakfast table and keep ice-cold drinks handy. Having a kitchen filled with guests or family during the preparation of a meal can be distracting and sometimes even disastrous (many a biscuit has burned under such circumstances), but these can also be the moments from which memories are made. "As a child, you wanted to be where your favorite person was, whether it was your mom or grandmother," says Stephanie Tyson, chef and co-owner of two Winston-Salem restaurants specializing in soul food. "If you had a cook, she was a trusted family member and probably a favorite with the children, as well."

The only Southern thing about kitchens below the Mason-Dixon Line that sport granite countertops, milled wood cabinets, and stainless-steel appliances may be the food that is cooked in them. But other homeowners choose a more regional look, with painted wainscoting or shiplapped boards applied to walls and ceilings that create a cozy, old-fashioned mood. Countertops, cabinetry, or ceiling beams of reclaimed heart pine add yet more warmth and a feeling of age, as does antique brick used in exposed chimneys dressed with country-carpenter-style mantels. Antique lanterns or rustic iron chandeliers retrofitted for incandescent lighting recall the days when kitchens were illuminated by candles, lanterns, and early tungsten lightbulbs. Fluorescent light has no place in the hospitable kitchen.

When asked what other ingredients an inviting kitchen should have, nearly all Southerners agree on cast-iron skillets, preferably old, well-seasoned ones. When used for cooking, they add flavor and evoke memories, conscious or not, of the people who prepared food in them over the years and served it to family and friends. Hung on walls or stacked on shelves, they have the same effect on their surroundings, seasoning them with the savory spice of life and friendship and love.

OPPOSITE: Interior designers Carter Kay and Nancy Hooff created this inviting dining area adjacent to the kitchen of a 1930s Atlanta, Georgia, house. Thomas McKenney and James Hall's nineteenth-century renderings of Native American chieftains add drama to the understated design of the space.

RIGHT: Ashleigh Goza left the two-tone painted plaster and enameled sink of the Depression-era kitchen of her early nineteenth-century plantation house untouched. Farm furniture combines with French-style zinc chairs and a Dutch-inspired chandelier to create a cozy space for family meals and casual entertaining.

PREVIOUS SPREAD: Interior designer Chuck Chewning illuminates his Savannah kitchen with a dramatic 1911 Thomas Edison fixture. Cabinets of knotty pine warm the dual-duty space where intimate dinners are often served with silver, etched glasses, and Ashworth Brothers Hanley ironstone china.

LEFT: William Bates dressed up his modest Charleston kitchen with marble backsplashes.

OPPOSITE: Architect Norman Askins prefers to conceal utlitarian objects like dishwashers and refrigerators in conveniently located butler's pantries.

FOLLOWING SPREAD, LEFT: Heirloom silver goblets dress up an antique French fruitwood table that serves as a place for both family meals and casual entertaining.
RIGHT: Architect Keith Summerour created this sunny dining alcove that complements the Colonial Revival style of a 1930s house in Atlanta, Georgia.

This easy-to-make and even easier-to-eat recipe from chef Stephanie Tyson's *Well Shut My Mouth!: The Sweet Potatoes Restaurant Cookbook* is a perfect kitchen-counter snack.

HOT COLLARD GREEN, BACON, AND BLUE CHEESE DIP

1 cup sour cream
½ cup freshly grated Parmesan cheese,
plus additional cheese for garnish
½ cup crumbled blue cheese
½ cup cream cheese
½ cup chopped cooked bacon
4 cups cooked collard greens, drained
¼ cup diced pimentos
Two dashes of Texas Pete Hot Sauce

Preheat the oven to 375°F.

In a large mixing bowl, combine the sour cream, ½ cup Parmesan cheese, blue cheese, cream cheese, and bacon. Squeeze the moisture from the greens and then roughly chop them. Add the greens and pimentos. Finish with about 2 shakes of Texas Pete.

Spray or oil the inside of a 2-quart casserole dish. Add the dip and sprinkle with a little Parmesan cheese. Bake for about 15 minutes, or until hot and bubbling.

RIGHT: Soothing shades of blue and pink introduced through wall paint, handmade porcelain, Indian napkins, and tulips warm the dining bay beside Susan Hable Smith's kitchen.

Into the Outdoors

—

GARDENS AND PAVILIONS

In the South, relaxation has always been a priority, in part because the hot climate makes it hard to do much more than sit in the shade and talk for many months of the year. Porches surrounded by greenery and fragrant climbing vines are one obvious place to pursue the art of doing very little, but the porch is just a springboard for living and entertaining in the surrounding landscape. The best way to entice your guests to step out into the great outdoors is to put something inviting within their immediate line of sight: a garden of heirloom roses trimmed with boxwood, a gazebo or decorative pool pavilion, or a weathered stone statue or neoclassical folly in the distance. A convivial stroll through a twilit garden, a morning cup of coffee on a secluded bench, or a festive meal beside the pool are among the memorable moments the host with a well-considered yard can offer, whether it's a postage-stamp courtyard or a grand estate.

"The pleasure of being in intimate outdoor spaces is very specific to the Southern genre of entertaining," observes Ben Page, landscape architect and past president of the Southern Garden History Association. "The idea of beautiful, encapsulated garden rooms is a legacy of English and Italian design, but Southerners made it their own by employing human-scaled proportions that encourage connectivity." The prevailing tradition is one of precision across the Atlantic. The profusion with which the South's trees and plants bloom and the speed at which they grow defies order, lending a romantic sensuality to even the most geometric scheme. Evergreen walls grow higher and flowering vines creep nearer, making garden spaces feel all the more like intimate rooms in the wild in the cool of dusk. The walled gardens of Charleston, Savannah, and New Orleans

PREVIOUS SPREAD: Inspired by English gardens, Helen Pruitt copied the Duchess of Beaufort's gazebo for serving tea and cocktails in her Charleston garden.

ABOVE: Hydrangeas provide a colorful backdrop for entertaining in the woodland garden of antiques dealers John Knowlton and Bob Davis. Mid-century wire garden furniture adds vintage charm.

OPPOSITE: Susan Hable Smith employs her favorite shade of pink in a rose arbor above a gate opening to her spacious yard.

have the same effect, summoning the feeling of being in a world apart. In *Mrs. Whaley and Her Charleston Garden*, published in 1997, Emily Whaley describes such a gathering—one of the alfresco black-tie dinner parties traditionally hosted by Charlestonians in the last week of April and first of May.

> *When we arrived the moon was just rising over the harbor and . . . as we went down to dinner in the garden, it had just cleared the rooftops and was flooding every corner with silvery light. The scene we came upon could have been taken from a hardly believable romantic dream. All of our senses were assailed at once. The fragrance of . . . Confederate jasmine, which is almost but not quite as heady as that of a gardenia, was a never-to-be-forgotten part of the evening. Flowering vines climbed up along the winding wrought-iron stairway to the long balcony above. A light breeze was stirring the white blossoms on the oleanders and . . . picked up the pale blue-gray smoke rising from the candles and wafted it upward into the deep blue moonlit-sky. The moon seemed to be ours alone.*

Chinese Chippendale pavilions, nineteenth-century English-style gazebos, and neoclassical pergolas and pool houses provide equally enchanting environments for afternoon tea, twilight cocktails, and outdoor dinners. But the South is also known for its

RIGHT: Hostesses Linda Heagy and Judy Powell set a lavish table in a garden shed of tabby and brick, resembling the historic outbuildings of Georgia's sea islands. Gilt palm tree–shaped candlesticks and china adorned with leaves mirror the garden setting.

ABOVE: Although newly constructed, this Saint Simons Island garden shed designed by architect John Shackelford recalls the ruins of nearby plantation outbuildings. Attached to the guesthouse, the structure easily accommodates both gardening pursuits and plein-air meals and twilight cocktail gatherings.

OPPOSITE: Philodendron leaves gathered from the surrounding tropical garden serve as place mats that complement the china's leaf green borders. The foliated pattern of etched wine glasses repeats the natural motif.

more rustic forms of entertaining, exemplified by the fire pits for barbecuing meats or roasting oysters found outside the finest country houses as well as the humblest ones. Outdoor entertaining was a favorite way to honor guests from afar, as an account from a nineteenth-century tourist from Virginia recalls. Describing a woodland barbecue prepared by a host of servants, John Duncan wrote, "One was preparing a fowl for the spit, another feeding a crackling fire which curled up round a large pot, others were broiling pigs, lamb, and venison over little square pits filled with red embers of hickory wood. From this last process the entertainment takes its name." Oyster roasts, first practiced by the indigenous people of the South, also became popular with colonists and are still enjoyed as traditional Thanksgiving and Christmastime feasts.

Whether it's a fire pit surrounded by plank benches, a garden bower, or a flowering courtyard, all outdoor entertaining spaces have a special allure. They incite the imagination in anticipation of a gathering that will possess that certain frisson of excitement reserved for parties out of doors. "When you can see a situation right there outside the door and window that is calling to you, it has everything to do with invitation," says architect Bobby McAlpine. "You can see it asking for a gathering which may or may not happen." If you are a Southerner, born and raised with a strong streak of hospitality, or a transplanted one, you will make sure that gathering happens and in a way your guests will never forget.

OPPOSITE: Interior designer Athalie Derse selected muted natural shades to adorn a slate-topped table in her Charleston garden. Mid-century chairs by Brown Jordan with paint matching the old brick foundation of her house, woven-grass place mats, and a centerpiece of ligularia cut from the garden blend into their surroundings.

LEFT: Floral artist Martha Reeves arranged flowers in a bark-sheathed wooden container for a garden club luncheon in Atlanta.

ABOVE, LEFT: Watermelon is the perfect summer treat, especially when displayed ceremonially on a raised silver platter from India. RIGHT: An old tin shed updated with domestic-style double-sash windows serves as a storage and potting shed, an occasional entertaining space, and a garden design studio for Holley Jaakkola.

OPPOSITE: Weathered French bistro furniture perched in a shady corner of the vegetable garden creates the perfect place for sharing a refreshing drink of water with a friend.

LEFT: With antique French garden cloches as pendant lights and a weathered worktable large enough to seat six, Holley Jaakkola's potting shed/studio is also ideal for serving summertime luncheons. Anna Weatherly china, hand painted in Hungary with water lilies, sets a fanciful table adorned with ceramic mushrooms and a loose arrangement of flowers in a matching soup tureen.

LEFT TO RIGHT: The best garden architecture issues an invitation to approach. Architect Bobby McAlpine designed a sequence of spaces beginning with a garden path passing through a columned seating area and terminating at the pool house. Charleston-based architect David Creech enclosed a courtyard with diminutive neoclassical structures. Landscape architect Glen R. Gardner created a dreamy alcove approached by stepping-stones. Roses and a perennial border soften this stone-bound garden bower designed by landscape architect Deanna Pope.

RIGHT: A rustic stone tower, wooden arch, white picket gate, and distant sundial demonstrate the many ways to transform a yard into an inviting garden. Each element beckons the guest to explore. Architect Bobby McAlpine often invokes a quality of romance in outdoor spaces with towers, dovecotes, and other folly-like structures.

ABOVE: Landscape architect Deanna Pope employed forced perspective by gradually narrowing the width of stone steps leading to a pool terrace with a neoclassical pavilion designed by architect Carolyn Laurens. Gently pruned boxwoods and a distant stone wall softened by climbing roses create a sense of drama and discovery.

OPPOSITE: French cast-limestone sphinxes of the early twentieth century guard the boxwood path leading through a Charleston garden designed by landscape architect Glen R. Gardner. The impression is a feeling of good fortune that you are invited to approach the table through the lush, semitropical setting.

OPPOSITE AND LEFT: Garden stairs and paths that may eventually lead to nowhere create a sense of mystery and progression. Implying that the pursuit may be more important than the destination, they invite garden strollers to appreciate their surroundings. Designed by landscape architect Deanna Pope, these pathways make the most of the hilly terrain and woodland character of the suburbs of Atlanta, Georgia.

ABOVE AND OPPOSITE: Pool pavilions offer infinite possibilities as illustrated
by these three examples. Architect Beau Clowney and designer Muffie Faith
channeled tropical sources in this pavilion with tall prop shutters. A pool pavilion
designed by architect Bobby McAlpine takes cues from local barn architecture
and Colonial Revival design. A rustic-chic pavilion designed by architect William
Litchfield for Atlanta interior designer Nancy Hooff taps woodland mountain style.

FOLLOWING SPREAD: From the brick and stone pavings to the boxwood-trimmed
water garden and the classical columns and balustrade of a lattice-walled pergola,
symmetry infuses every aspect of this garden entertaining area designed by
Nashville-based landscape architect Ben Page.

RESOURCE GUIDE

ARCHITECTURE

Norman Davenport Askins
normanaskins.com
(404) 233-6565

Beau Clowney
beauclowney.com
(843) 722-2040

David A. Creech
creech-design.com
(704) 609-1987

Tim Cuppett
cuppettarchitects.com
(512) 450-0820

D. Stanley Dixon
dsdixonarchitect.com
(404) 574-1430

William B. Litchfield
litchfielddesigns.com
(404) 467-4600

Carolyn Llorens
carolynllorens@me.com
(404) 307-5415

Bobby McAlpine
mcalpinehouse.com
(844) 624-6633

John P. Shackelford
jpshackelford.com
(912) 634-0924

Alison Spear
alisonspear.com
(845) 298-0888

Jim Strickland
historicalconcepts.com
(678) 325-6665

Keith Summerour
summerour.net
(404) 603-8585

Ken Tate
kentatearchitect.com
(985) 845-8181

DESIGN

William Bates, designer
williambatesdesign.com
(646) 456-8859

Jill Biskin, artist
jillbiskin.com
(706) 254-0761

Susan B. Bozeman
interior designer
sbbdesigns.com
(404) 237-7745

Charles H. Chewning
interior designer
chuckchewning.com
(404) 723-8167

Bob Christian, artist
bobchristiandecorativeart.
com
(912) 234-1960

Athalie Derse
interior designer
athalie@me.com
(847) 528-8595

Landy Gardner Interiors
landygardner.com
(615) 383-1880

Susan Hable Smith
artist and designer
hableconstruction.com
susanhablesmith@gmail.com

Rosemary James
interior designer
faulknerhousedesigns.com
(504) 586-1609

Carter Kay
interior designer
Nancy Hooff,
interior designer
carterkayinteriors.com
(404) 261-8119

Jenny Keenan
interior designer
jennykeenandesign.com
(843) 452-9053

Jacquelynne P. Lanham
interior designer
jackyelanham.com
(404) 364-0472

LANDSCAPE AND GARDEN

Glen Gardner
landscape architect
gardnerla.com
(843) 772-5885

Erica Goza
flower farmer
and floral designer
branchingoutsc@gmail.com
(864) 934-2875

Holley Jaakkola
floral and garden design
holleyjaakkola@yahoo.com
(912) 441-4824

Candace Brewer Long
landscape architect
candacelong@winstream.net
(912) 242-2219

Ben Page
landscape architect
pageduke.com
(615) 320-0220

Deanna Pope
landscape architect
Pope Garden Design
(404) 403-3122

Martha Reeves
floral designer
graciousnest.com
(404) 402-9746

CULTURAL ANTHROPOLOGY

Dawn Corley
silver expert
thecharlestonsilverlady.com
(843) 568-5425

Dale L. Couch
curator of decorative arts,
Henry D. Green Center
for the Study of the
Decorative Arts
dcouch@uga.edu

Lee Epting
events planner
eptingevents.com
(706) 353-1913

Matt Lee and Ted Lee
authors
mattleeandtedlee.com
(843) 720-8890

Scott Peacock
chef, author,
documentarian,
and biscuit maker
Black Belt Provisions
chefscottpeacock.com

Stephanie Tyson, chef
Sweet Potatoes Restaurant
sweetpotatoes.ws
(336) 727-4844

SHOPPING

The Atlanta Decorative
Arts Center
adacatlanta.com
(404) 231-1720

Fritz Porter
fritzporter.com
(843) 207-4804

The Horseshoe Crab
thehorseshoecrab.com
(912) 920-2404

John Knowlton Antiques
jknowltonantiques.com
(706) 248-7507

John Pope Antiques
johnpopeantiques.com
(573) 230-1666

Leontine Linens
leontinelinens.com
(504) 899-7833

The Paris Market
theparismarket.com
(912) 232-1500

SOUTHERN HOME FINDERS

Lois Lane
Charleston
loislaneproperties.com
(843) 806-1055

Janet Miller
Savannah
janet.miller@
sothebysrealty.com

BIBLIOGRAPHY

A very special thanks is due to the librarians of the Charleston Library Society, established in 1748 and the second-oldest circulating library in America, for helping me discover primary historical accounts of hospitality in the old South.

Breaux, Daisy. *Favorite Recipes of a Famous Hostess*. Washington: Polytechnic Publishing Co., 1945

Carmichael, Virginia. *Porches and Portals of Old Fredericksburg, Virginia*. Richmond, VA: Old Dominion Press, 1932.

Chamberlain, Samuel. *Southern Interiors of Charleston*. New York: Hastings House, 1956.

Fant, Jennie Holton, ed. *The Travelers' Charleston: Accounts of Charleston and Lowcountry, South Carolina, 1666–1861*. Columbia, SC: The University of South Carolina Press, 2016.

Henderson, Mary F. *Practical Cooking and Dinner Giving: A Treatise Containing Practical Instructions in Cooking; In The Combination and Serving of Dishes; And in the Fashionable Modes of Entertaining at Breakfast, Lunch and Dinner*. New York: Harper & Brothers, Publishers, 1881.

The Junior League of Charleston, comp. *Charleston Receipts*. Charleston, SC: The Junior League of Charleston, 1950.

The King's Daughters, comp. *Suggestions for Charleston Tea*. Charleston, SC: Press Deutsche Beitung, c. 1906.

Lee, Matt, and Ted Lee. *The Lee Bros. Charleston Kitchen*. New York: Penguin Random House, 2013.

Rhett, Blanche H., Lettie Gay, and Helen Woodward. *200 Years of Charleston Cooking*. New York: Jonathan Cape and Harrison Smith, Inc., 1930.

Taylor, John Martin. *Hoppin' John's Lowcountry Cooking, Recipes and Ruminations from Charleston & the Carolina Coastal Plain*. New York: Bantam Books, 1992.

Tyson, Stephanie. *Well Shut My Mouth!: The Sweet Potatoes Restaurant Cookbook*. Winston-Salem, NC: John F. Blair Publisher, 2011.

————. *Soul Food Odyssey*. Winston-Salem, NC: John F. Blair Publisher, 2015.

Whaley, Emily, and William Baldwin. *Mrs. Whaley and Her Charleston Garden*. Chapel Hill, NC: Algonquin Books, 1997.

————. *Mrs. Whaley Entertains*. Chapel Hill, NC: Algonquin Books, 1998.

ACKNOWLEDGMENTS

There are many ways to say thank you—with a smile, garden flowers, a handwritten note, even with an email, I'm told, although I always feel guilty. But the best way to say thank you is in the pages of a book. With that in mind, I start by acknowledging my longtime publisher at Rizzoli International Publications, Charles Miers, and friend and editor Sandy Gilbert Freidus, for believing in my vision and bringing it to beautiful fruition. Heartfelt gratitude is offered to my graphic designer, Jan Derevjanik, for the artistic eye and loving patience she brought to this project. And what would I do without copyeditor Elizabeth Smith, with whom I share my words with trust and gratitude? Immense gratitude goes to historian Jennie Holton Fant, whose research of eighteenth- and nineteenth-century accounts for *The Travelers' Charleston* were invaluable. I am always indebted to those who help open doors for me and special thanks are due to Hal Williamson of New Orleans, who introduced me to Peggy Galis of Athens, Georgia, who opened several more doors of houses featured here. Sister house-lover Janet Miller of Celia Dunn Sotheby's International Realty in Savannah also opened doors to many charming residences, including her own. Thank you! An equally enthusiastic thanks is offered to Atlanta interior designer Susan Bozeman, who led me to several gracious homes. Mint juleps, cheese straws, and bonbons galore are offered to all the home-owners, as well as their architects, landscape architects, and interior designers, who shared their vision of Southern hospitality with my readers and me.

PAGE 204: The lyre-shaped arm of a Directoire settee adds a curvaceous silhouette to an early nineteenth-century paneled living room illuminated by crystal candelabras.

OPPOSITE: Mirrored panels and modern sconces update the walls in the living room of a simple Greek Revival summer house.

ABOVE: Details that introduce an element of surprise, such as this hand-painted plate, encourage guests to pause in the hall before moving on to the entertaining rooms.

First published in the United States of America in 2019 by
Rizzoli International Publications, Inc.
300 Park Avenue South
New York, NY 10010
www.rizzoliusa.com

Copyright © 2019 Susan Sully
Photography: Susan Sully
with the exception of the following photography:
Reed Brown, pp. 202–203
Timothy Dunford, pp. 24–25, 68, 94, 116
J. Savage Gibson, pp. 58, 130
Matt Harrington, p. 95
Julia Lynn, pp. 12, 131, 200
Simon Upton, pp. 192, 194–195

Publisher: Charles Miers
Editor: Sandra Gilbert Freidus
Design: Jan Derevjanik
Production Manager: Colin Hough Trapp
Managing Editor: Lynn Scrabis

Printed in China

2019 2020 2021 2022 / 10 9 8 7 6 5 4 3 2 1

ISBN: 978-0-8478-6363-1
Library of Congress Control Number: 2019937995

Visit us online:
Facebook.com/RizzoliNewYork
Twitter: @Rizzoli_Books
Instagram.com/RizzoliBooks
Pinterest.com/RizzoliBooks
Youtube.com/user/RizzoliNY
Issuu.com/Rizzoli

RIGHT: A rickety cabinet filled with gardening books and miscellanea provides additional serving space when designer Holley Jaakkola entertains in her garden shed.

CAPTIONS FOR THE FOLLOWING IMAGES:
Cover and title page Small chairs invite cozy conversation in the sunny bay window of artist Susan Hable Smith's nineteenth-century Georgia home.

p. 4–5 Veils of Spanish moss sway from the limbs of live oak trees, forming a living hallway linking a nineteenth-century Charleston, South Carolina, plantation house with the banks of the Ashley River.

p. 6 Old Paris porcelain and a Chinese export tureen add color to a classic Sunday dinner setting laid with English silver and perfectly pressed linens on a polished mahogany table.

p. 8 The colonnade spanning the facade of this nineteenth-century vernacular Greek Revival farmhouse endows it with welcoming, unpretentious charm.

p. 11 A vibrant tablescape of pink lusterware, etched glasses, antique silver, and bright Indian napkins gets the conversation started in Susan Hable Smith's dining room.

p. 12 A sequence of doors, colors, and patterns invites you to enter and enjoy the variously sheltered spaces of this Sullivan's Island, South Carolina, beach house designed by architect Beau Clowney.

p. 19 China in the Indian Tree pattern has been popular in the South from the late eighteenth-century to the present, in part because it dresses up and down with equal ease.

Endpapers, Cargo wallpaper from Andrew Martin International (distributed by Kravet) features the blue-and-white china that was shipped by the barrelful to Southern ports in the eighteenth and nineteenth centuries. For an array of fabrics and wallpapers ideal for the hospitable Southern home, visit Kravet.com.